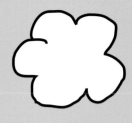

Some Days I Flip My Lid

Learning to be a Calm, Cool Kid

Kellie Doyle Bailey, MA, CCC-SLP, MMT

Illustrated by Hannah Bailey

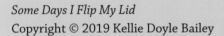

Published by:
PESI Publishing & Media, Inc.
3839 White Ave.
Eau Claire, WI 54703

Illustrations: Hannah Bailey
Cover: Hannah Bailey
Layout: Mayfly Designs & Amy Rubenzer

Library of Congress Control Number:2019948979

ISBN: 9781683732518
Printed in Canada

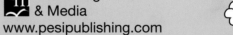
PESI
Publishing
& Media
www.pesipublishing.com

My name is Max and I am 8. I'm in the 3rd grade and some days are great!

On days that are great
my brain feels just right.

I had a yummy
breakfast and I slept
through the night.

When my brain is just right,
I can listen and learn.
I'm okay in school and
I don't feel concern.

But then there are days that don't go so well, because

SOME DAYS I FLIP MY LID.

Flipping my lid means I lose my cool and my learning gets tricky when I'm in school.

This can happen on days when I don't sleep just right because I tossed and I turned in my bed all night.

I toss and I turn when I'm worried or sad, embarrassed, confused or just plain mad.

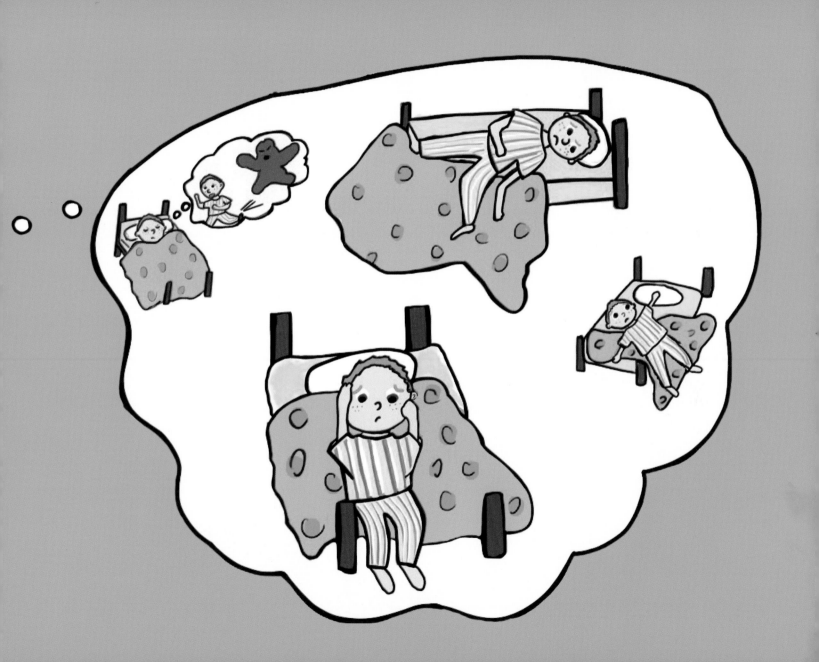

When I **FLIP MY LID** things happen to me that can change how I learn and listen and see.

My face gets blotchy and my body feels tight.

I say mean things and I sometimes fight.

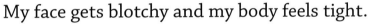

My knees get wobbly and I can't breathe.

I want to run away or sometimes I freeze.

Do these things ever happen to you?
Do you **FLIP YOUR LID?**
Do you **LOSE YOUR COOL?**

On days when I get **MAD**
I flip my lid and I **FIGHT**.

It's never okay and it never
feels right.

When I fight I'm like a tiger
and I'm ready to spring.
I roar with my words when
my friend wants the swing.

I really don't like it when I fight.
My brain feels tense and my
fists get tight.

After I fight, I still feel mad,
so flipping my lid only
makes me feel bad.

My Mom says tigers aren't allowed in school.

She says I need to be calm and cool.

Are you ever mad when you're at school?
Do you **FLIP YOUR LID?**
Do you **LOSE YOUR COOL?**

Some days I **FLIP MY LID** when
I'm confused or upset.
I sit in my seat and I worry and fret.
On days like this, my brain isn't okay.
I just want to run or fly far away.

Running away is also called **FLIGHT.**

I do this on days when my head feels too light.

When I'm in flight, I'm like a balloon, I soar high and free.

I bounce in the air above the tall trees.

Subtraction:

32
− 23

I really don't like when I fly.
When I settle back down,
I just want to cry.

After a while, my balloon
shrinks and it pops.
I'm still confused and upset
and the worry won't stop.

My Mom says balloons aren't allowed in school.
She says I need to be calm and cool.

Are you ever confused when you're at school?

Do you **FLIP YOUR LID?**

Do you **LOSE YOUR COOL?**

Then there are days when
I'm a little afraid.
My belly feels jittery and
it doesn't go away.

When I'm afraid, I just
want to **FREEZE**.
My heart starts to pound
and I'm weak in the knees.

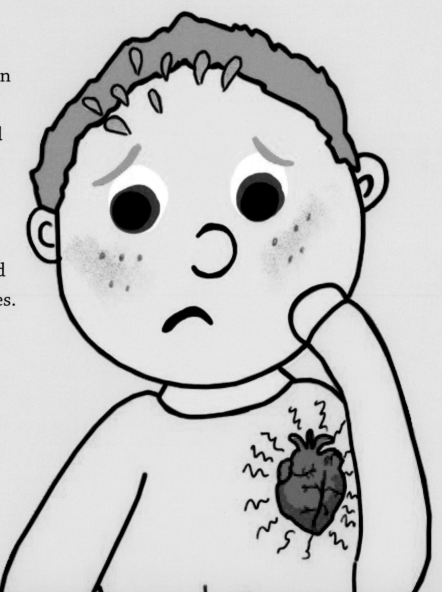

My Mom says snowmen aren't allowed in school.
She says I need to be calm and cool.

Are you ever afraid when you're at school?

Do you **FLIP YOUR LID?**

Do you **LOSE YOUR COOL?**

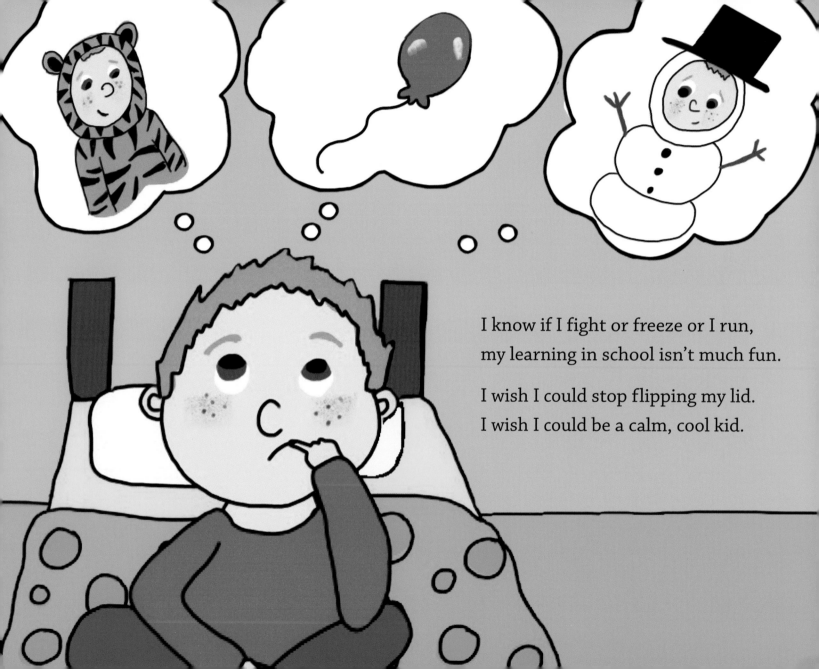

I know if I fight or freeze or I run,
my learning in school isn't much fun.

I wish I could stop flipping my lid.
I wish I could be a calm, cool kid.

Then one day, Mom and I took a walk.
We sat by a pond and we had a nice talk.
She told me we all have days when we're sad,
or scared or worried or just plain mad.

She said flipping my lid is not a good way
to learn and grow in school each day.

Mom taught me a new way to deal when I fret, so I won't flip my lid when I'm scared or upset.

It's called **MINDFUL BREATHING** and it's pretty cool. It's a way to calm down when I'm home or in school.

Mom said it's a choice if I fight,
run or freeze.

I can choose calm and cool
whenever I please.

FYI:
SUBSTITUTE
TEACHER
TOMORROW ☺

It helps me relax and it can be done in my seat.

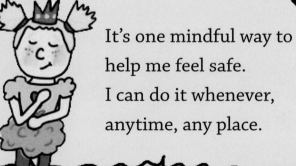

It's one mindful way to help me feel safe.
I can do it whenever, anytime, any place.

Here's how I do it, here's how it's done.
It all begins with breath number one.

I'm still while I breathe, that's part of the fun.
This helps me settle so I don't want to run.

I focus my eyes on just one place.
I breathe in and out while the red leaves my face.
I breathe in and out as my eyes open wide, then
my body and brain can calm down inside.

Taking three **MINDFUL BREATHS,**
a few moments each day, helps me stay
focused in a whole new way.

Taking three **MINDFUL BREATHS**
stills my brain and my heart, which is a
really good place for my learning to start.

Remember … Some days are tricky and other days are fun, but no matter what, we can choose not to run. We can decide not to fight or fly away too, because breathing on purpose keeps our brain calm and cool.

WOULD YOU LIKE TO TRY IT TOO?

NOTE TO TEACHERS

So many of our students who we are blessed to teach are approaching their learning from a place of reactivity. This is especially true for students who suffer from trauma, anxiety, symptoms of ADHD, sensory dysregulation and executive function difficulties. Teaching students to become responsive rather than "reactive learners" is an important social and emotional tool for self-awareness and self-management.

We can teach all our students that there are different ways to handle life stresses. Teaching children about the brain and especially this concept of "flipping our lids" can support them in their ability to notice their body, heart and brain when life situations get too big or scary. Mindfulness is a great way to help your students learn strategies to become Calm, Cool Kids.

Mindfulness in education is sweeping the nation as an invaluable tool for helping our children become responsive learners. Current brain research shows that children who learn to be present and self-regulate at a young age, have better social-emotional learning outcomes in schools. In fact, social-emotional intelligence is the number one factor in a child's success in life and even trumps IQ! Mindfulness is one way to help bring this awareness to our young learners and help them to be successful and independent communicators and life-long learners.

Mindfulness is simple and easy to do and can help all students become present in your classroom. By definition, mindfulness means being right here, right now with curiosity and interest and without judgment. Teaching students to be present and curious while feeling safe and loved is a gift and a blessing.

There are a variety of mindful activities that can be taught in brief moments each day. Mindful breathing is a good first place to introduce this concept. Teaching children to pay attention to their breathing helps to build self-awareness of their breath and, as a result, works to calm their central nervous systems and regulates their minds and bodies for just-right learning.

HERE'S HOW TO DO IT

* Invite your students to sit in a Mindful Body Posture (in their seats, face forward, feet resting on the floor in front of them; trunks are tall and straight like a giraffe; neck is long and shoulders, neck and face are relaxed).

* Present a soothing tone using a chime or bowl or soothing bell.

* Invite your students to close their eyes or look at something directly in front of them (remind them that if they look at one another this might make them giggle so focus on an object if they aren't comfortable closing their eyes). Just a reminder that children who suffer from trauma or abuse may not feel safe closing their eyes; this is not a requirement.

* While listening to the beautiful tone, lead the class in taking three slow, deep breaths.

* Encourage your students to pay attention, on purpose, to their breathing until the tone ceases.

* Invite the class to open their eyes or refocus on you when they are ready.

* Thank your students for taking this Breath Break.

* Lead the class in a conversation about how the classroom feels when they are taking Mindful Breaths (i.e., peaceful, calm, quiet, focused, safe, relaxed, etc.).

* Encourage your students to take a Breath Break for themselves whenever they notice that they are getting ready to Flip Their Lids (when they feel hot in their face, tight bodies, itchy ears, eyes can't see; when they want to fight, fly away or freeze).

* Consider incorporating 3-5 Breath Breaks each day into your classroom routine and watch with curiosity as your students become Calm And Cool.

NOTE TO PARENTS AND CAREGIVERS

Being a kid is tricky and the rigors and demands for learning life are real. Each child learns at different rates and stages so it's really important for them to know how to recognize the signals for "flipping their lids."

I invite you to use this book as a starting point for conversations with your child as they begin to understand the lid-flipping signals (red face, heart racing, tight arms and legs, ears that whoosh and eyes that aren't focused) when they are mad, upset, overwhelmed or sad. Take the time to explore these feelings with your child and explain that these same things happen to big people too. Some days we feel like flipping our lids, but it's very important to have the skills to stay calm and cool.

Mindful breathing is one great way to help us to calm our heart, body and mind. Consider beginning each day with a moment of mindful breathing - it's a perfect way to help everyone start the day feeling safe, loved and connected. Practicing mindful breathing before going to sleep at night helps unwind from all the busyness of being a kid.

May You Be Well –

Kellie Doyle Bailey
MA, CCC-SLP, PC
Mindfulness & SEL Educator

ACKNOWLEDGEMENT

I was inspired to write *Some Days I Flip My Lid* after spending the past
several years teaching children about the brain and using Dr. Dan Siegel's
Hand Model of the Brain for Flipping Your Lid. Dr. Siegel is a brilliant clinical
professor of psychiatry at UCLA School of Medicine and the founding
co-director of The Mindful Awareness Research Center at UCLA. For
more information about Dr. Siegel's work, please visit www.drdansiegel.com

AUTHOR

Siveleaf photography

KELLIE DOYLE BAILEY, MA CCC-SLP, MMT, is the proud mother of Hannah and Doyle who have been her best life teachers. She is a veteran speech-language pathologist of 28 years and a certified mindfulness mediation teacher. Kellie works in public schools in Mid Coast Maine collaborating with K-8 grade educators to help children learn how to be Calm, Cool Kids. She teaches mindfulness in education at The University of Maine in Farmington and provides workshops and trainings across Maine. She lives in Northport, Maine with her husband Bruce.

ILLUSTRATOR

Siveleaf photography

HANNAH G. BAILEY, BA, recently graduated from The University of Maine in Orono, with a teaching certification in Art Education. She currently works with children with diverse needs and implements mindful practices daily to assist with keeping her kids calm and cool. Hannah is pursuing her masters in school counseling as well as her mindfulness meditation certification.